**Penguin Readers**

THE BOY IN THE STRIPED PYJAMAS

JOHN BOYNE

LEVEL

RETOLD BY ANNA TREWIN
ILLUSTRATED BY DAVID SHEPHARD
SERIES EDITOR: SORREL PITTS

PENGUIN BOOKS

UK | USA | Canada | Ireland | Australia
India | New Zealand | South Africa

Penguin Books is part of the Penguin Random House group of companies
whose addresses can be found at global.penguinrandomhouse.com.
www.penguin.co.uk www.puffin.co.uk www.ladybird.co.uk

The Boy in the Striped Pyjamas first published by David Fickling Books Ltd, 2006
This Penguin Readers edition published by Penguin Books Ltd, 2020

007

Original text written by John Boyne
Text for Penguin Readers edition adapted by Anna Trewin
Text copyright © John Boyne, 2006
Illustrated by David Shepard
Illustrations © Penguin Books Ltd, 2020

The moral right of the original author has been asserted

Printed and bound in Great Britain by Clays Ltd, Elcograf S.p.A.

A CIP catalogue record for this book is available from the British Library

ISBN: 978-0-241-44742-0

All correspondence to
Penguin Books
Penguin Random House Children's
One Embassy Gardens, 8 Viaduct Gardens,
London SW11 7BW

MIX
Paper | Supporting
responsible forestry
FSC
www.fsc.org
FSC® C018179

Penguin Random House is committed to a
sustainable future for our business, our readers
and our planet. This book is made from Forest
Stewardship Council® certified paper.

Contents

People in the story   4

New words   5

Note about the story   6

Before-reading questions   6

Chapter One – Change   7

Chapter Two – Out-With   12

Chapter Three – Stupid Father   20

Chapter Four – An accident   26

Chapter Five – Grandmother leaves the party   30

Chapter Six – The boy in the striped pyjamas   33

Chapter Seven – Lieutenant Kotler comes to dinner   40

Chapter Eight – An imaginary friend   45

Chapter Nine – A surprising visit   49

Chapter Ten – Hair lice   54

Chapter Eleven – Leaving Out-With   59

Chapter Twelve – Together at last   64

During-reading questions   70

After-reading questions   72

Exercises   73

Project work   77

Glossary   78

People in the story

Bruno

Maria

Father and Mother

Gretel

Adolf Hitler

Pavel

Lieutenant Kotler

Shmuel

New words

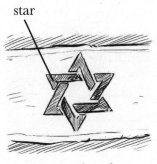

star

armband

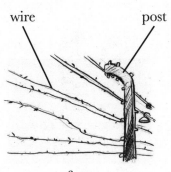

wire   post

fence

shaved head

striped pyjamas

swing

uniform

Note about the story

The Boy in the Striped Pyjamas is about Bruno, a boy from Germany, during the Second World War. At this time, Germans were very angry. They lost the First World War in 1919 and many other countries were not happy with Germany and its people. The country was also very poor and many German people thought this was because of immigrants – people who came from other countries – and **Jews***. Adolf Hitler became Germany's leader in 1934. (Germans called Hitler "the Führer", which in German means leader, but Bruno hears this word as "fury" – which means *very angry* in English.)

Bruno's father is an important person in the German army. One evening, Hitler comes for dinner and gives Bruno's father a very important job. He will be the **Commandant** of Auschwitz (which Bruno hears as "Out-With") in Poland, a place where in the war, millions of Jews were kept and killed.

The terrible story which follows is told through Bruno's young eyes. Bruno does not understand what is happening at Auschwitz. He believes everything that his parents tell him and often remembers their words – these words are shown in CAPITAL letters.

Before-reading questions

1 What do you know about Adolf Hitler and the Nazis?

2 The boy in the story, Bruno, lives near Auschwitz. What do you know about Auschwitz? What happened there?

*Definitions of words in **bold** can be found in the glossary on pages 78–79.

CHAPTER ONE

Change

One afternoon, Bruno came home from school and was surprised to find Maria, the family's **maid**, in his bedroom. She was **packing** his clothes and his things in large boxes.

"What are you doing, Maria?" he asked as **politely** as possible because his mother always told him never to be **rude**. "Please don't touch my things!"

But Maria shook her head and then pointed to Bruno's mother, who was standing at the top of the stairs. She was a tall woman with long red hair that she wore in a ball on top of her head. She held her hands together tightly and was watching Bruno with a worried face.

"Mother!" said Bruno. "What is happening? Why is Maria packing my things?"

"Come downstairs with me," replied Mother, so he followed her down to the family's large dining room.

He looked around it and remembered that his parents and the Fury, and the Fury's friend Eva, were sitting here a week ago. His father was wearing his new **uniform** and he looked very **proud**.

"Who is the Fury?" Bruno remembered quietly asking his sister, Gretel, while they watched the four adults.

"He is the **leader** of Germany, stupid! And that's his girlfriend, Eva," Gretel replied. "They've come for dinner with Mother and Father!" she added, proudly.

Bruno remembered that the Fury was much shorter than Father and not as strong. He had dark hair and had a strange small square of black hair above his mouth. The woman with him was very beautiful. She had blonde hair and a red mouth, and she smiled a lot.

Then Bruno and Gretel came into the dining room and Father introduced them to the Fury. "These are my children, Fury," he said. "Gretel and Bruno."

"Which one is which?" replied the Fury, and laughed. But Bruno did not think this was very funny.

"I'm twelve and he's nine," explained Gretel. "I can speak French."

"Why do you want to speak French?" asked the Fury, and he laughed again. Then he sat down in Father's chair and Bruno remembered thinking that this was very rude. Mother's face was red when she asked Lars, their cook, to bring the soup. Then she told the children to go upstairs.

The Fury and Eva stayed for more than two hours. Bruno and Gretel were not invited to say goodbye to them. Bruno watched them leave from his bedroom.

"What a horrible, rude man," he remembered thinking.

Later that night, Bruno heard some of Mother and Father's conversation in Father's office.

" . . . to leave Berlin for a place like that . . . " Mother was saying.

" . . . we cannot choose . . . my work must continue . . . " replied Father.

" . . . we cannot let them live near a place like that . . . " said Mother again.

" . . . and I don't want to hear another word about it!" shouted Father.

And now, a week later, something strange was happening and Bruno guessed that it was because of the Fury's visit. Bruno sat at the dining room table and looked at his mother. He noticed her white face and red eyes.

"You must not worry, Bruno," she said. "It's going to be an adventure."

"Am I going away?" asked Bruno.

"Not just you," she replied. "We are all going away. Your father and I, Gretel and you. All four of us."

Bruno thought about this and **frowned**. He did not really want Gretel to come because she WAS A LOT OF TROUBLE FROM THE BEGINNING. He knew this because his parents often said it.

"But where?" he asked. "Where are we going? Why can't we stay here?"

"We have to leave here because of your father's job," explained Mother. "You know how important it is, don't you, Bruno?"

"Yes, of course," said Bruno. He knew that lots of people came to the house because of Father's job. Men in wonderful uniforms came and secretaries, too. Everyone was very **polite** to Father. "He's an important man," he heard them say. "The Fury has big plans for him."

But Bruno was not sure what job Father actually did. At school, his friends often talked about their fathers. Bruno knew that Karl's father worked in a shop, and Daniel's father was a teacher. But when his friends asked about Bruno's father, he just said, "Father is an important man and the Fury has big plans for him. And he wears a wonderful uniform."

"We must leave because Father will be **lonely** in his new job without us," Mother said now. "You don't want Father to be lonely, do you?"

"We'll have to close the house for now," replied Mother. "We will come back to it one day."

"But what about Lars and Maria?" asked Bruno.

"They're coming with us," explained Mother.

"Where are we going?" he said. "Is it more than a mile away?"

Mother **sighed** again. Then she laughed a little. "Yes, Bruno. It is more than a mile away. A lot more."

Bruno's eyes opened wide and his mouth opened. "So we're leaving Berlin?" he said.

"Yes," Mother replied. "Your father's job is . . . "

"But what about school?" cried Bruno. "And what about Karl, Daniel and Martin? How will they know where I am?"

"You'll have to say goodbye to them for now," said Mother. "But I'm sure that you'll see them again later. And please be polite, Bruno," she added. "Do not talk when I am talking."

"Say goodbye to them?" said Bruno, and he was nearly shouting now. "Say *goodbye* to them?"

"You'll make other friends," said Mother. "I'm sorry Bruno, but we don't have . . . "

"But Mother . . . !"

"Bruno, that's enough!" she **snapped**, and then she stood up. "Now go upstairs and help Maria with your packing."

CHAPTER TWO
Out-With

When he first saw the new house, Bruno's eyes opened wide and his mouth made the shape of an O. Everything about it was the opposite of their house in Berlin and he could not believe that they were really going to live there.

The house in Berlin had five **floors**. It stood on a quiet street next to other big houses which also had boys living in them. And around their street were lots of other streets full of more large houses and cafés and a fruit and vegetable market. But their new house only had three floors. It stood alone in an empty, wide area and there were no other houses near it. This meant that there were no other families near and no other boys for Bruno to play with. When he closed his eyes he felt that he was in the loneliest place in the world.

"I think that this was a bad idea," said Bruno to Mother a few hours after they arrived while Maria was unpacking his boxes. Maria was not the only maid at the new house – there were three others now who were very thin and only spoke very quietly. There was also an old man called Pavel, who **prepared** the vegetables for lunch. He looked unhappy and a bit angry.

"We did not choose to come here," replied Mother and frowned. "Somebody decided for us." When Mother said "somebody", she usually meant Father.

"I think that this was a bad idea," Bruno said again.

"Bruno, I want you to go upstairs and help Maria unpack, and I want you to do it now!" snapped his mother.

Bruno went upstairs with a pain in his stomach. He wanted to cry, but he stopped himself. He felt that everything was wrong. How did this happen? One day he was happy at home, playing with his friends. The next day he had to stay here in this cold, unfriendly house with three thin maids and an angry, unhappy old man.

"Mother sent me to help," he said to Maria.

Maria nodded and pointed to a big bag with his clothes in it. "You can **sort** those **out**," she said.

Bruno sighed and began sorting out the clothes. "What do you think about this, Maria?" he said after a few minutes. He liked Maria and felt that she was one of the family.

"What do I think about what?" asked Maria.

"This," he said. "Coming to a place like this. Have we made a big mistake?"

"I can't answer that," said Maria. "You know about your father's job."

"But I don't want to move away from our house and my friends, and . . . "

At that moment, Bruno stopped speaking because he heard a noise. He looked at the door of Mother and Father's room. Suddenly a man came out. He was younger than Father and not as tall, but he wore the same uniform. Under his **cap**, he had blonde hair, and he was carrying a box. When he saw Bruno, he looked the boy up and down, then frowned. Then he went downstairs.

"Who was that?" asked Bruno.

"One of your father's soldiers," replied Maria.

"I don't think that I like him," said Bruno. Then he added, "I don't think that there's anyone to play with here, Maria. There's only Gretel and she WAS A LOT OF TROUBLE FROM THE BEGINNING."

Bruno felt like crying again and turned towards the wall. He did not want to look like a baby in front of Maria. He looked around the room for something interesting, but there was nothing. Then he suddenly noticed something.

In the corner of the room, opposite the door, there was a long, high window. Bruno moved over to it and looked out. Maybe he could see Berlin and his house from here? He put his face to the glass and his eyes opened wide and his mouth made an O again. He could see something that made him feel very cold and very unsafe.

Bruno knew that Gretel WAS A LOT OF TROUBLE FROM THE BEGINNING. His parents often said it because she did a lot of BAD THINGS. She was always in the bathroom for hours and she had too many dolls. Bruno felt that her dolls watched him when he went into her room. Her friends were also not very nice and they often laughed at Bruno. So that was one good thing about leaving Berlin – her friends did not come to the house any more.

This morning, Bruno ran into Gretel's room without knocking and saw her dolls sitting around the room.

"What are you doing in here?" shouted Gretel. "You must knock first!"

"Did you really bring all your dolls here?" asked Bruno, without answering her question. He sat down on her bed.

"Of course I did," replied Gretel. "We will be here for some time."

"How long is 'some time'?" asked Bruno. "Weeks? A month?"

"I think weeks," said Gretel. "Maybe three."

"That's all right then," said Bruno. "I don't want to stay a month. I hate it here."

Gretel looked at her little brother and nodded. "It's not very nice, is it?"

"It's horrible," said Bruno.

"Well, yes," agreed Gretel, "but the house can be made nicer. Then it won't be so bad. I heard that the last people who lived at Out-With left very quickly. They didn't have time to make the place nice for us."

"Out-With?" asked Bruno. "What's an Out-With?"

"It's not *an* Out-With, Bruno," said Gretel. "It's just Out-With. It's the name of this house."

"But what does it mean?" Bruno asked. "Out-With what?"

"I don't know," said Gretel, and she picked up one of her dolls. "Now please get off my bed. You're making it untidy."

Bruno jumped off the bed. "I **miss** Karl, Daniel and Martin," he said.

"And I miss Hilda, Isobel and Louise," replied Gretel.

"I don't think the other children look friendly," said Bruno, quietly.

Gretel immediately put down the doll and turned to look at him. "What *other* children?" she asked. "I haven't seen any other children."

Bruno looked around the room. There was a high window here, too, but Gretel's room was on the other side of the house from his. Bruno smiled and began to walk towards his own room.

"What other children?" said Gretel again, following him. "Where are they?"

Bruno entered his room and went to the window. He heard her come and stand behind him. "They're out there," he said, and pointed.

Gretel slowly moved forward and looked out. It was a bright sunny day, and the sun came out from behind a cloud. At that moment, she saw what Bruno was talking about. But they were not all children. Some were adults and some were old people. So they were children, fathers, uncles, grandparents. They were *everyone*.

"Who are they?" asked Gretel. "Where are all the girls?"

"I don't know," said Bruno. "Maybe they live in a different part. But it's not as nice as home."

Gretel agreed. She did not want to look, but it was difficult to look away. There was a nice garden under Bruno's window, which had flowers in it and a **wooden** seat. But after that everything changed. Then there was a huge **wire fence** which ran past the house and continued for many miles. The fence was very high – higher than their house – and it had lots of tall wooden **posts**. There was no grass on the other side of the fence, only **mud**, and then there were lots of narrow, wooden buildings.

"You see?" said Bruno. He was happy because Gretel could only see the people from his bedroom window and not hers. This meant that the people were *his*.

"I don't understand," said Gretel. "What a horrible place. Who are all those people and what are they all doing there?"

Everywhere they looked they could see people. Tall, old, short, young and all moving around. Some were in groups, some were alone. There were soldiers behind the wire, too. Sometimes they followed the people, and the people began to run. Then the soldiers laughed.

"I told you," said Bruno. "See, there are children here."

"They're not children that I want to play with," said Gretel. "They look *very* dirty."

"Maybe they can't have baths," replied Bruno.

Gretel watched for a few more minutes, then she turned away. "I'm going back to play with my dolls," she said. But when she got back to her room she sat on her bed and thought about the people behind the wire.

Bruno stayed at the window watching the people. "How strange!" he said. Because he suddenly noticed something. All the people that he could see – the boys, the men, the grandfathers – they were all wearing the same grey **striped pyjamas** and grey **striped cloth** caps on their **shaved heads**.

"How very strange!" he said to himself again. Then he slowly turned away.

CHAPTER THREE

Stupid Father

Bruno decided to speak to Father. He quickly went down to Father's office and saw him standing inside with a group of five men. They were laughing and shaking hands. Father was in the middle and he looked very important in his new uniform. Bruno felt quite frightened of him. The other men's uniforms were not as new or as clean, and they all held their caps in their hands. They called Father "**Commandant**".

" . . . he made mistakes," one of them was saying.

"The Fury had to do it,' said a different man. "The numbers weren't enough . . . "

Father suddenly **lifted** his arm in the air and the men went silent. "Thank you for your kind words," he said. "The past is finished. This is a new beginning. But at the moment I must be with my family. It is all very new here for them and I don't want any trouble!"

The men all laughed and shook his father's hand again. Then they lifted their arms, too and said two words which Bruno knew very well. He knew that when anyone said the words to him, he had to say them back. Then the men all left and Father went back into his office, closing the door behind him.

In Berlin, Bruno had to STAY OUT OF FATHER'S OFFICE AT ALL TIMES. He only went in it once or twice, when Father had to HAVE WORDS with him about being naughty. He guessed that it was the same here at Out-With. But he really wanted to speak to Father and so he quietly knocked on the door.

"Enter!" said a voice.

Bruno pushed the door open and moved inside. Then his mouth made the shape of an O. The rest of the house was dark and boring, but this room was different. It had high walls and tall windows, and lots of books. In the middle was a huge wooden desk. Father was sitting behind the desk and he looked up from some papers when Bruno entered. When he saw his son, he smiled.

"Bruno," he said, coming around the desk and shaking the boy's hand. "My boy," he added, after a moment.

"Hello, Father," said Bruno, quietly.

"Please sit down," Father said, then he went back to his side of the desk. Bruno sat down in a big armchair.

They were both silent for a few seconds, then Father smiled again and said, "So what do you think?"

"What do I think?" answered Bruno. "What do I think of what?"

"Of your new home. Do you like it?"

"No," Bruno said, quickly. "I think we should go back to Berlin."

Father looked down at his papers but he kept smiling. "Out-With is our home now," he said after a moment. "Home isn't just a building. Home is where the family are, isn't it?"

"But when can we go back to Berlin?" asked Bruno. "It's much nicer there. Grandmother and Grandfather are there and they're our family, too."

Father nodded his head. "But you, Mother and Gretel are the most important people in our family and this is where we live now. At Out-With. Please don't look so unhappy about it, Bruno."

"But Karl and Daniel aren't here and there are no other houses or shops or streets or cafés," cried Bruno. "And there's no fruit and vegetable market."

"Bruno, sometimes there are things we have to do in life and this is one of them," Father explained, tiredly. "This is my work, important work. One day you'll understand."

"Well, I don't think that you can be very good at your job if we have to live here," replied Bruno.

"Go to your room, Bruno," Father replied in a quiet voice which frightened him. The boy got up and walked towards the door. Then he stopped and turned around.

"Father?" he began.

"Bruno, I'm not going to . . . "

"It's not that," said Bruno, quickly. "I have another question."

Father sighed. Then he nodded.

"Who are all those people outside?" asked Bruno.

Father looked a bit **confused** at Bruno's question. "They are soldiers," he said. "And secretaries. And lots of people who work for the Fury."

"No, I mean the people behind the big fence. They're all wearing the same clothes."

"Ah, *those* people," said Father, nodding again because now he understood. "Well, they're not really people at all, Bruno."

"They're not?"

"No, Bruno. And you must not worry about them. They're not like you at all. Please just try to like your new home and be good. I'm not asking for anything more."

"Yes, Father," said Bruno, but he did not feel happy about this answer. Then he lifted his arm in the air and said those two important words, "*Heil Hitler*".

"Everyone says that, so maybe it means 'Goodbye'," he thought as he left the office, "or 'Have a nice afternoon'."

A few days later, Bruno was lying on his bed and looking at the dirty walls in his bedroom.

"Everything is horrible," he said loudly to himself. "I hate this house. I hate it all. I'm so bored."

At this moment, Maria came in through the door carrying his clean clothes. "Good morning," she said quietly and then she started sorting out his shirts and trousers.

"I'm sure that you hate this new house, too, Maria," Bruno said. She turned to look at him strangely, like she did not understand what he said.

"Don't you like it here then?" she asked.

"Like it?" he replied, and laughed. "*Like* it? Of course I don't like it. It's awful. There's nothing to do. There's no one to talk to or play with."

"I enjoyed the garden at the house in Berlin," said Maria, and then she sighed. "The flowers were very beautiful and they smelled so nice."

"So you don't like it here then?" asked Bruno.

"It's not important what I think," said Maria.

"Of course it's important," replied Bruno. "You're part of our family, aren't you?"

"I don't know about that," replied Maria, but she smiled at his words.

"I think that coming here was a mistake. Stupid Father."

Maria's eyes opened wide and she moved towards him with her hand over her mouth. "You must not say that about your father," she said. "He is a good man and he has done many things for me." Then she sat on the bed and continued quietly. "You don't remember how I came to work for you, do you? How could you? You were only three years old."

Bruno frowned. Maria was just the family maid. He never thought of her as a person with a life and a past. But of course she thought about things, and like him she had friends that she missed and wanted to see again.

"My mother knew your father when he was a boy," she explained. "She worked for your grandmother when she was a singer in theatres. They were friends for many years. But times were difficult and my mother became ill and had to go to hospital. Your father paid for everything, and he took me into his house and gave me a job. So don't call your father stupid, Bruno." She stood up and looked worriedly out of the window at the people in the striped pyjamas. "He is a good man, so I really don't understand why he . . . "

But the sound of a car door closing made her silent. Then Gretel came running up the stairs. When she saw Maria in Bruno's room, she stopped and frowned.

"Run me a bath, Maria," she said.

"Why can't you run yourself a bath?" snapped Bruno.

"Because she's the maid," said Gretel. "That's what she's here for."

CHAPTER FOUR
An accident

"If I don't find something interesting to do soon, I'll go crazy," Bruno thought after three weeks at Out-With.

So one Saturday afternoon, he decided to make himself a **swing**. A hundred metres from the house there was a tall tree which looked strong enough to hold a small boy. Now he just needed some **rope** and an old tyre. The rope was easy to find because there was lots of it in the garage. He took a knife and cut some, then carried it to the tree.

Neither Mother nor Father was at home on this day, so they could not help him. There were lots of soldiers' trucks near the house – this was normal – but he knew that it would be impossible to steal a tyre from any of them.

Then he saw Gretel in the garden talking to Lieutenant Kotler – the young man that Bruno saw when he first arrived at the house. He often visited them now. Bruno decided, unhappily, that he was the best person to ask. He walked towards them and said hello.

"What do *you* want?" said Gretel.

"Good morning, Little Man," said Lieutenant Kotler. He always called Bruno this and the boy hated it.

"I wanted to ask if there were any tyres around that no one needs," said Bruno. "On one of the trucks, maybe?"

"Of course," said Lieutenant Kotler. "What do you want it for?" He was not wearing his uniform today and he looked much younger than usual. Gretel was watching him with her big eyes and smiling at everything he said.

"I want to make a swing," Bruno said.

Lieutenant Kotler stared at him for a moment, then turned round. He noticed Pavel, the old man who prepared the vegetables, walking towards the house.

"Hey, you!" Lieutenant Kotler shouted, and then said a word which Bruno did not understand. "Come over here, you —"

Pavel came towards them and Lieutenant Kotler spoke to him rudely. "Take this little man to the **shed** at the back of the house. There are some old tyres in it. He will choose one and you will carry it for him." Then he used the same word to Pavel again, "Do you understand, you dirty —?"

Pavel held his cap in his hands and nodded.

"Go on then," said Lieutenant Kotler, and Bruno followed Pavel towards the shed, but he was unhappy about leaving his sister with the young soldier. Lieutenant Kotler was not a nice man.

———

The accident happened a few hours later. Bruno was **swinging** happily on the tyre when he kicked the tree and the tyre turned. Then he felt himself fall and everything went black for a moment. He woke up in Pavel's arms. The old man was carrying him into the kitchen.

"I don't know what happened," Bruno said.

"You were going too high," Pavel replied. He put him down carefully on one of Mother's wooden chairs and

27

looked carefully at his knee. "Now don't move for a moment and don't worry. It's only a small cut."

Bruno frowned and watched while Pavel got a box from the cupboard and started taking things out of it. He stopped the blood and cleaned Bruno's cut. Then he covered it with a **plaster**.

"There," he said. "Now you need to sit here quietly for a few minutes. Don't go near that swing again today."

Bruno nodded. "Thank you," he said. "Do you think that I should see a doctor? It might be worse than you think."

"It's not," said Pavel, and he moved to the **sink**.

"Well, how do you know?" asked Bruno and frowned. "You're not a doctor."

Pavel started silently washing some carrots with his head down. Then he looked across the kitchen at Bruno.

"Yes, I am," he said. "Before I came here, I worked as a doctor. I was a very good one, too."

Bruno looked back at him, confused. "But you're a waiter," he said. "You prepare the vegetables. How can you be a doctor, too?"

Just at that moment, Mother entered the kitchen. As soon as he heard her, Pavel looked back down at the sink and continued to wash the carrots.

"What happened to you?" said Mother, seeing Bruno's plaster.

"I made a swing and then I fell off it," Bruno replied. "And then the swing hit me on the head. Pavel carried me in and cleaned my cut. Then he put this plaster on me. It hurt, but I didn't cry once, did I, Pavel?"

Pavel moved a little but he did not lift his head. "The cut is clean," he said. "There's nothing to worry about."

"Go to your room, Bruno," said Mother.

Bruno got off the chair and left the room, but he was still able to hear Mother say "Thank you," to Pavel. Then he heard her say, "If the Commandant asks, we'll say that I cleaned Bruno's cut."

CHAPTER FIVE
Grandmother leaves the party

The two people that Bruno missed the most were
Grandfather and Grandmother. They lived together in a
small flat near the fruit and vegetable market. Grandfather
was seventy-three, and he owned a restaurant in Berlin.
He did not work there any more, but he visited it every day.
He liked sitting at the bar and talking to the customers.

Grandmother could never be an old woman in Bruno's
eyes. In the past, she sang at the theatre. She was beautiful,
and she had long red hair and green eyes like his mother's.
When they had parties, Grandmother always sang lots
of songs. Bruno loved listening to her. And at Christmas,
Grandmother always brought strange clothes for him and
Gretel to wear and they all acted little **plays** together.

The plays were usually lots of fun, but the last one went
very wrong and Bruno still remembered it. A week before
it happened, the Fury came for *that* dinner with Eva, and
Father started wearing his new uniform. Grandfather
was proud of his son when he saw the uniform, but
Grandmother was very angry.

When Bruno and Gretel finished their play,
Grandmother sat down and looked sadly at Father.

"What did I do wrong with you, Ralf?" she said.
"You think that uniform makes you special and you don't
care what it means."

"This is a party, Mother," said Father. "And it's Christmas. Please don't talk about this now."

"I'm happy and proud to see him wearing it," said Grandfather. "He's helping to make his country better again after so many bad things were done to it!"

"Oh, please listen to yourselves!" cried Grandmother. "Which one of you is the most stupid?"

"But Nathalie," said Mother, "don't you think that Ralf looks handsome?"

"Handsome!" shouted Grandmother. "Handsome, did you say? Do you think that is the most important thing? You stupid girl!"

"Go upstairs, children," said Mother, quickly. "Go to your rooms."

31

Bruno and Gretel got up and slowly walked up the stairs. A few minutes later, Bruno heard Grandmother shouting in the hall. "When I look at that uniform, I want to pull my eyes out of my head," she cried. Then she shut the door hard behind her. It was the last time that Bruno saw her.

The weeks passed and not much changed at Out-With. But Bruno did not remember Karl and Daniel's faces quite so well now and Berlin did not feel so close.

The soldiers came to speak to Father in his office every day, and then left. Lieutenant Kotler visited a lot too, and when he wasn't with Father, he was usually outside talking with Gretel. She always laughed loudly at his jokes and played with her hair while she listened to him. This made Bruno angry. The other maids moved quietly around the house, and Pavel too, but he and Bruno never spoke about the accident.

But then things changed. Father decided that the children needed to study and he paid a **tutor** called Herr Liszt to come to the house. So Bruno and Gretel now had lessons every morning and afternoon. Bruno thought that Herr Liszt was strange. He was friendly most of the time, but there was a strange look in his eyes and inside he seemed angry.

Herr Liszt liked **history**, while Bruno liked reading stories and art. "Those things are not important," said Herr Liszt. "You must understand who you are and where you came from. You must learn about your great country and the bad things which were done to it and to you."

CHAPTER SIX
The boy in the striped pyjamas

A few days later, Bruno was sitting in his bedroom and thinking about all the things he liked doing in Berlin that he was not doing at Out-With. Most of them needed friends and he did not have any. And Gretel did not want to play with him.

But there was one thing he did in Berlin and he could do it here, too. That was **exploring**.

"When I was younger," Bruno said to himself, "I loved exploring. I've not done any exploring here. Maybe it's time to start."

Bruno immediately jumped off his bed and found a coat and an old pair of boots. Then he left the house and walked through the bright sunny garden towards the long wire fence. He wanted to know who the strange people in the striped pyjamas were. What was it all about?

Behind the fence, it was like a city. All the people working and living together next to the house where he lived. "What's different from Berlin?" he thought. "And which person decides who wears the pyjamas and who wears the uniforms?" He knew that the soldiers left this house and went to the people in the striped pyjamas. So why did they never bring them back to their house for dinner?

Bruno reached the fence and looked to his right. The tall posts and wires continued on and on and he could not see where they stopped. But that was fine for an **explorer**. Bruno began to follow the fence, feeling like Christopher Columbus, who was Bruno's favourite explorer. He walked and walked, and each time he looked back at his house, it was smaller than the last time. While he was walking, he never saw anyone close to the fence.

An hour passed and he began to feel hungry. "Maybe that's enough exploring for one day," he thought. But then he noticed something small and dark. He looked hard to try and see what it was.

His feet kept moving, taking him closer and closer until he suddenly realized that the small dark thing was a boy. The boy was just sitting there, looking at the ground. Bruno slowed down and then, when he reached the boy, he stopped.

"Hello," he said.

"Hello," said the boy, looking up.

He was smaller than Bruno. He wore the same striped pyjamas as all the other people on that side of the fence and he had a cloth cap on his head. He wasn't wearing any shoes or socks and his feet were dirty. He wore an **armband** which had a star on it.

"Are you exploring?" asked Bruno.

"Are you?" said the boy. Bruno noticed that the skin on the boy's face was grey and his eyes were enormous and very sad.

"Yes," said Bruno. "For two hours now."

"Have you found anything?" asked the boy.

"Well, I found you," Bruno replied, after a moment. Then he sat down opposite the boy and looked at him through the wire. He wanted to ask why the boy looked so sad, but decided not to yet.

"I live in the house on this side of the fence," he explained. "It's only got three floors. My room is on the first floor and I can see over the fence from there. My name's Bruno."

"I'm Shmuel," said the little boy. "I've never heard of your name."

"And I've never heard of yours," replied Bruno.

"There are lots of Shmuels here," said the boy.

"How old are you?"

"I'm nine," replied Shmuel. "My birthday is 15th April and I was born in 1934."

Bruno's eyes opened wide and his mouth made the shape of an O. "I don't believe it!" he said. "My birthday is 15th April, too, and I was born in 1934. We were born on the same day. Isn't that strange?"

"Very strange," said Shmuel.

Bruno suddenly felt very happy. A picture of Karl and Martin and Daniel came into his head.

"Do you have many friends?" he asked.

"Oh, yes," said Shmuel. "Well, some. There are a lot of young boys here. We fight a lot of the time, though. That's why I come here. To be alone."

"It's not fair," said Bruno. "Why am I on this side of the fence where there's no one to play with and you've got lots of friends that you can play with? I must speak to Father about it."

"Where did you come from?" asked Shmuel.

"Berlin," Bruno replied. "It's in Germany. Don't you come from Germany?"

"No, I'm from Poland," said Shmuel. "But I speak German because Mother teaches it in school. She teaches French and Italian, too."

"Poland," said Bruno, slowly. "That's not as good as Germany, is it?"

Shmuel frowned. "Why isn't it?" he asked.

"Well, because GERMANY IS THE GREATEST COUNTRY IN THE WORLD," Bruno replied, remembering Father's words. "So where is Poland?"

Shmuel was silent for a moment, and then he said, "This is Poland."

"Is it?" asked Bruno, looking surprised.

"Yes," said Shmuel. "But it's not a very nice part of it."

"Berlin is much nicer," said Bruno. "We had a big house there with five floors and there were lovely streets with cafés and a fruit and vegetable market."

"Kracòw, where I come from, is nicer than Berlin," said Shmuel. "Everyone is very friendly and the food is much better, too."

"Well, we don't agree, but that's OK," said Bruno, because he did not want to fight with his new friend. Then he asked, "Why are there so many people on that side of the fence and what are you all doing there?"

Shmuel was quiet for a moment, then he said, "All I know is this. Before we came here, we lived in a small flat over a watch shop – where Father makes his watches. We were happy. Then one day things started to change. I came home from school and my mother was making this armband for me, with this star," and he pointed to the band on his arm. "We had to wear it when we went outside."

"My Father wears one on his uniform, too," said Bruno. "It's very nice. I'd like one."

"But they are different, aren't they?" said Shmuel, shaking his head. "We wore the armbands for a few months, and then things changed again. We had to leave our house . . . "

"That happened to me, too!" shouted Bruno. "The Fury came for dinner, and then we had to move here. I hate it here. Did he come to your house, too?"

"No. We had to move to a different part of Kracόw and the soldiers built a big wall. We all had to live in one room with another family. There were eleven of us and the mother and father kept fighting."

"Gretel likes fighting," started Bruno. "She's . . . "

"We lived there for some months," continued Shmuel, who did not seem interested in Gretel. "Then one day the soldiers came with huge trucks. Lots of people didn't want to leave. They ran away or hid under the floors. The truck took us to a train and the train brought us here. It was a terrible journey. There were too many of us and there was no air. The smell was terrible. When the train stopped, we got out and had to walk here."

"We had a car," said Bruno.

"Then Mother was taken away from us," said Shmuel, "and Father and I were put in those long buildings."

Shmuel looked very sad when he finished this last sentence, but Bruno did not know why. It did not seem that terrible. Nearly the same thing happened to him.

"You don't have any food, do you?" asked Shmuel.

"I'm sorry," said Bruno. "I wanted to bring some chocolate, but I forgot."

"Chocolate . . . " said Shmuel, very slowly.

Bruno suddenly stood up. "I should go back," he said. "Maybe you could come to dinner with us one evening?"

"Maybe," said Shmuel.

"Or I could come to you. I could come and meet your friends."

"You're on the wrong side of the fence," said Shmuel.

"I could get under it," replied Bruno. "There's a bit of wire that's broken here," and he lifted up the wire from the ground. It made a hole that a small boy could easily get through.

Shmuel stood up and started to move away. "I have to go back," he said.

"I'll come back tomorrow," shouted Bruno, but Shmuel said nothing. Then he turned and started to run back to the buildings.

Bruno started walking home. As he walked, he decided not to tell anyone about his new friend. They might not like Bruno coming here. No, he would make it his secret – well, his and Shmuel's.

CHAPTER SEVEN

Lieutenant Kotler comes to dinner

Week after week followed, and Bruno slowly understood that they were not going back to Berlin. He had to forget about playing with his friends. It slowly became harder to remember Karl and Daniel, and the cafés and fruit and vegetable market. But life was not so bad at Out-With because now he had a new friend to talk to. Every afternoon, after his classes, he took some bread from the kitchen and hid it under his coat. Then he walked along the fence and talked to Shmuel until it was time to come home.

"I'm sorry I'm late," he said one afternoon when he found Shmuel sitting on the ground waiting for him. "I was talking to Maria."

"Who's Maria?" asked Shmuel.

"She's our maid. She's very nice, though Father says she's PAID TOO MUCH. But I was talking to her about Pavel. He's a waiter and he prepares our vegetables. I think that he lives on your side of the fence."

"On my side?" asked Shmuel.

"Yes," said Bruno. "Do you know him? He's very old and wears a white jacket when he brings us dinner. He's from Poland, too – like you. You've probably seen him."

"No," said Shmuel, shaking his head. "There are a lot of people on this side of the fence. There are thousands of us and most are from Poland."

"Well, I thought you might know him," Bruno continued. "He was a doctor before he came here. He cleaned my cut but Father must not know or there will be trouble."

"The soldiers don't usually like people getting better," said Shmuel.

Bruno nodded, but he did not know what Shmuel meant. He looked up at the sky and was quiet for a moment. Then he said, "What do you want to be when you're older?"

"Yes," said Shmuel. "I want to work in a zoo because I like animals."

"I'm going to be a soldier," said Bruno. "Not a bad one like Lieutenant Kotler, but a good one like Father."

"There aren't any good soldiers," said Shmuel.

"Father is a good soldier," said Bruno.

Shmuel did not answer. Both boys went quiet for a few minutes. Then Shmuel said in a low voice, "You don't know what it's like in here."

"You don't have any sisters, do you?" asked Bruno, quickly. "You're lucky. Gretel thinks she knows everything but she WAS A LOT OF TROUBLE FROM THE BEGINNING. She's always outside with Lieutenant Kotler and laughing at his jokes."

Bruno noticed his friend's face was white.

"What's wrong?" he asked.

"I don't like talking about him," Shmuel said. "He frightens me."

"He frightens me, too," said Bruno. "He's not very nice to people."

Shmuel began to shake a little.

"What's the matter? Are you cold?" Bruno asked. "Why didn't you bring a sweater? The evenings are getting colder."

When Bruno got home he was unhappy because Lieutenant Kotler joined the family for dinner. Bruno watched Pavel while he moved around the table with the wine bottle and felt sad for him. He seemed to get smaller and thinner every week. "Is his white jacket the same as the one he wore when he was a doctor?" Bruno thought.

After Pavel put the plates on the table with shaking hands, he stood back and did not move at all. His eyes looked very tired and wet and Mother had to ask twice for her soup.

"Herr Liszt doesn't like books or the theatre," said Bruno, eating his meal. "He only wants us to study history. I'm starting to hate history. It's so boring."

"Don't say 'hate', Bruno, please," said Mother.

"Boring?" said Father. "My son thinks that history is boring? Let me tell you . . . " Father moved forward in his chair and held his knife up. "History is why we are sitting in this house. It's why we are here and not in Berlin. History is making the wrong things that were done to us right."

"I enjoyed history when I was at school," said Lieutenant Kotler. "My father taught art at the university, but I preferred history."

"I didn't know that, Kurt," said Mother. "Does he still teach there now?"

"I don't know," replied Kotler. "He left Germany in 1938. We don't speak much."

Father stopped eating for a moment and frowned. "And where did he go?" he asked.

Kotler's face turned a little red. "I think he is in Switzerland," he said, "teaching at Berne University. We're not close."

"And why did he leave Germany when his country needed him most?" asked Father. "Was he ill and needed the good air of Switzerland? Or did he run away from the war? But maybe this is not the right time to talk about it."

Father suddenly turned and called for more wine. "What's wrong with you tonight?" he asked Pavel, angrily. "This is the fourth time I've had to ask for wine."

Bruno watched the old man try to open the bottle with his shaking hands. He filled Father's glass, but as he turned to fill Lieutenant Kotler's, he dropped the bottle. It fell on Kotler's legs.

What happened then was terrible. Lieutenant Kotler became very angry with Pavel and no one – not Bruno or Gretel or Mother or even Father – tried to stop him from what he did next.

Later when Bruno went to bed, he thought about Pavel and what happened at dinner. He remembered how kind Pavel was to him when he had his accident and how he cleaned his cut. He knew Father was a kind man, so why didn't he stop Lieutenant Kotler from getting so angry with Pavel?

If that was the kind of thing which happened at Out-With, Bruno decided, then he must not make any trouble. Somebody did not like it.

CHAPTER EIGHT
An imaginary friend

Bruno continued to meet Shmuel after his lessons with Herr Liszt. His mother usually went to sleep in the afternoon and never noticed him leave. And Gretel was normally in her room playing with her dolls.

Shmuel was usually waiting for him in the same place, staring at the ground. One afternoon, Bruno noticed that he had a **bruise** around his eye. But when Bruno asked him about it, he just shook his head. "I don't want to talk about it," he said.

Bruno still wanted to go under the fence to play with his friend and the other boys. He asked about it every day. But every day Shmuel said no, it was not a good idea. "I don't know why you want to come here anyway," he added one afternoon. "It's not a very nice place."

"You haven't lived in my house," Bruno replied, forgetting Shmuel's story of eleven people living in one room before they came to Out-With. "It doesn't have five floors, only three. It's so small!"

Another day he asked, "Why do you all wear the same striped pyjamas and caps?"

"That's what they gave us when we arrived here," explained Shmuel. "They took away our other clothes."

"But don't you sometimes wake up in the morning and want to wear something different?"

Shmuel opened his mouth to say something and then closed it again.

"I don't even like striped clothes," said Bruno.

A few days later, Bruno woke up and saw that it was raining heavily. It continued falling through breakfast and through his lessons with Herr Liszt. When they finished in the afternoon, it was still raining. This was bad news because it meant that he could not meet Shmuel.

Bruno lay on his bed with a book but it was hard to read because he kept thinking about Shmuel. At that moment, Gretel came in to see him. She did not usually come to his room. She preferred to play with her dolls.

"What do you want?" he asked.

"That's not nice," said Gretel. "I've got nothing to do. I hate the rain."

Bruno did not really understand this. His sister did not often leave the house. She did not go exploring like him and make new friends. How did the rain change this? But still, he was bored, too. "There are times," he thought, "when a brother and sister can stop their war. And this is one of those times."

"I hate the rain, too," he said. "I should be with Shmuel now. He will think that I've forgotten him."

The words came out before he could stop them. He suddenly felt very angry with himself.

"You should be with who?" asked Gretel.

"I'm sorry," said Bruno, slowly. "I didn't hear you."

"Who are you talking about?"

"Are you crazy?" he asked.

"What did you say, Bruno?" said Gretel in a low voice, and she lifted a hand and pointed a finger at him.

Bruno thought for a moment. He and his sister were both children, and she did not have friends either. Only her dolls. Maybe she was lonely at Out-With, too. But Shmuel was his friend and he did not want to share him. He could only do one thing – he had to lie.

"I do have a new friend," he began, slowly. "I go and see him every day, and he is waiting for me now. But you can't tell anyone about him."

"Why not?"

"Because he's not real. He's an **imaginary** friend," said Bruno. "We play together every day."

Gretel opened her mouth and then started to laugh. "An imaginary friend?" she said. "Aren't you a bit old for one of those?"

Bruno looked at the ground and tried to look like he was feeling stupid. He wanted his face to go red like Lieutenant Kotler's face at dinner when he spoke about his father in Switzerland.

"An imaginary friend," Gretel said again. "Really, Bruno! So what do you and your imaginary friend do together?"

Bruno smiled then because he knew that she believed him. Then he thought about it and he decided that he really did want to talk about Shmuel.

"We talk about everything," he said. "I tell him about our home in Berlin and he tells me about his family and his

47

father's watch shop and his old friends. But he doesn't have friends now because they were taken away."

"He doesn't sound much fun," said Gretel, and laughed.

"He hasn't seen his grandfather for a few days and he's very worried about him. His father keeps crying and holding him very hard."

Bruno stopped because he knew that these things were true. But at the time that Shmuel said them, Bruno did not really understand that his friend was feeling very sad. He suddenly felt terrible because every time Shmuel spoke about these things, he started talking about other things – small, stupid things.

"I'll say sorry for that tomorrow," he thought.

"Bruno, you must stop talking to imaginary friends or Father will think that you are mad," Gretel said.

Bruno nodded. "But I don't want to stop," he replied.

"Well, don't tell Father about it," she said.

"I won't," he said, "Now please go away. I want to read my book."

CHAPTER NINE

A surprising visit

The rain continued on and off for the next few weeks and Shmuel and Bruno could not meet as often as before. When they did meet, Bruno worried that his friend was getting thinner and thinner. His face was also very grey.

Sometimes Bruno brought bread and cheese to give to Shmuel, and sometimes a piece of chocolate. But often Bruno got hungry on the journey and ate a bit of the bread or chocolate. Then he wanted to eat more and more – until there was none left.

It was Father's birthday soon and Mother was planning a party. She invited lots of the soldiers at Out-With and worked hard to prepare for it. Bruno noticed that Lieutenant Kotler was always with her when she made her plans.

On the morning before the party, Bruno was reading in his room when he heard Lieutenant Kotler arrive at the house and speak to someone. A few minutes later, Bruno heard his mother talking about the party. He picked up his book *Treasure Island* and went downstairs. At the same time, Lieutenant Kotler came out of the kitchen.

"Hello, Little Man," the soldier said, with an unkind look in his eyes. "Where are you going?"

"Hello," said Bruno, frowning. Then he pointed at the living room. "I'm going in there to read my book."

Lieutenant Kotler quickly took the book from Bruno's hands and started to look through it.

"So what's it about?" he asked.

"Well, there's an island," replied Bruno, slowly.

"Yes, I guessed that," said Kotler. Then he held the book high and Bruno jumped but could not reach it.

At that moment Mother came through the kitchen door. "Kurt, my love, you're still here," she said. "I have some free time now if . . . Oh, Bruno, what are you doing here?"

"I'm going to the living room to read my book. Or I'm trying to . . . " replied Bruno, taking his book back from Lieutenant Kotler.

"Well, go in the kitchen for now," she said. "I need to speak with Lieutenant Kotler." And then they both moved into the living room and closed the door.

Bruno walked into the kitchen, feeling very angry, and suddenly he got the biggest surprise of his life. There at the table was Shmuel. Bruno could not believe it.

"Shmuel!" he said. "What are you doing here?"

"Lieutenant Kotler brought me. I have to clean the glasses," he said.

And when Bruno looked down, he saw sixty-four small glasses. Next to them was a bowl of hot water and a **cloth**.

"They needed someone with small fingers," Shmuel added, and he held out a very thin hand. Bruno held out his, too and saw for the first time how thin Shmuel's hand was next to his.

"How different our hands are!" said Bruno.

"My hand was like yours before," said Shmuel. "I don't know how it changed."

Bruno did not want to look at Shmuel's hand any more, so he went to the fridge and opened it. He was pleased to see some cold chicken in it. He took a knife and cut himself some large pieces, then he turned back to his friend.

"Are you hungry?" he asked.

"You don't have to ask that question," replied Shmuel.

"I'll cut some for you."

"No, if Lieutenant Kotler comes back . . ." said Shmuel, shaking his head and looking towards the door. "I'm only here to clean the glasses."

"It's only food," said Bruno, putting the chicken in his hand. "Just eat it."

The boy looked at the door for a moment, then quickly pushed the food into his mouth with frightened eyes.

At that moment, Lieutenant Kotler appeared through the kitchen door and stopped when he saw the two boys talking. Shmuel quickly reached for another glass and began cleaning it.

"What are you doing?" shouted Lieutenant Kotler. "I brought you here to clean the glasses, not talk."

"I'm sorry, sir."

"Have you got food in your mouth?" asked Lieutenant Kotler.

Shmuel shook his head.

"You *have* got food in your mouth!" shouted Lieutenant Kotler. "Did you steal something from that fridge?"

"No, sir. He gave it to me," said Shmuel, trying not to cry. He looked at Bruno. "He's my friend."

"Your . . . ?" began Lieutenant Kotler, looking confused. "What do you mean, he's *your friend*?"

Then he also turned to look at Bruno. He was silent for a moment. Then he said, "Do you know this boy, Bruno?"

Bruno's mouth opened and he tried to remember how to say "yes". He could see that Shmuel was very frightened and he wanted to make things better. But he could not because he was very frightened, too.

"I . . . He was here when I came in," said Bruno. "He was cleaning glasses."

"I didn't ask you that," replied Lieutenant Kotler, and now his voice was very angry. "Have you seen this boy before? Have you talked to him? Why does he say that he's your friend?"

"I've never spoken to him," said Bruno, quickly. "I've never seen him in my life. I don't know him."

Lieutenant Kotler nodded slowly and seemed happy with this answer. He turned back to Shmuel, who was looking at the floor.

"You will finish cleaning all these glasses," said Lieutenant Kotler in a low voice. "After that I will come to get you and take you back. Then we will talk about what happens to boys who steal. Do you understand me?"

Shmuel nodded and he picked up another glass with shaking hands.

Lieutenant Kotler turned to Bruno. "Come on, Little Man," he said, putting an unfriendly arm around his shoulders. Then Bruno heard the same bad word that Kotler used before with Pavel. "You go to the living room and finish your book. Leave this little — to finish his work."

CHAPTER TEN
Hair lice

Every afternoon after that day, Bruno went back to his and Shmuel's place at the fence, but his friend was not there. He began to think that what he said was too terrible and that Shmuel could not **forgive** him. But on the seventh day, he saw his friend sitting there, waiting for him.

"Shmuel!" he said, running to him and sitting down. "Shmuel, I'm so sorry. I don't know why I said it. Please forgive me!"

"It's all right," said Shmuel, looking up at him. Then Bruno saw the terrible bruises on his face. "What happened to you?" he said. "Did you fall off your bike? That happened to me back in Berlin two years ago. Does it hurt?"

"I can't feel it any more," said Shmuel.

"I'm sorry about last week," said Bruno. "I hate Lieutenant Kotler. I can't believe that I didn't tell him the truth. I'm so sorry."

When he heard that, Shmuel smiled and Bruno knew that he was forgiven. Then Shmuel lifted the wire and took Bruno's hand. The two boys smiled because they were touching for the first time.

It was now nearly a year since the family came to Out-With. Bruno did not think about Berlin and his friends there very much now. But then Grandmother died and the family had to go home. Those two days were very sad. Bruno knew that this was the end of Grandmother's songs and plays at Christmas.

Bruno was almost happy when they came back to Out-With. The house felt like his home now. He did not feel so angry about the three floors and the soldiers who came and went all day. Mother and Father seemed happier now and Mother did not go and sleep every afternoon. And best of all, Lieutenant Kotler was not at Out-With and no one called him "Little Man" now. Kotler left suddenly after a lot of shouting one night between Mother and Father. (Gretel was very sad, of course.)

But the very best thing in his life was Shmuel. He enjoyed walking along the fence every afternoon to see him. His friend also seemed happier. His face was not so grey, but he was still very thin. Bruno still talked about wanting to play with Shmuel, or going exploring with him. "Maybe one day we will," replied Shmuel. "If I can ever leave here."

Bruno started thinking more and more about the wire fence and the strange wooden buildings. He thought about talking to Mother or Father about them, but he did not want them to get angry. So he decided to ask Gretel.

He found her in her bedroom, and noticed that the dolls were not there. After Lieutenant Kotler left, she decided that she did not like them any more. Now she had maps of Europe on the walls and newspapers next to her bed.

"What do you want?" she snapped.

"I want to ask you something."

"Well, be quick."

"It's about Out-With . . . " he began.

"Bruno, it's not called Out-With," she replied. And then she told him how to say its real name.

"Well, I want to know about the fence," he said. "Why is it there?"

Gretel turned round in her chair and looked at him.

"You really don't know?" she asked.

"No," he replied. "I don't understand why we can't go to the other side. Why can't we play with the children there?"

Gretel looked at him for a moment, and then she began to laugh. "Bruno," she said, "the fence isn't there to stop us going to them. It's there to stop them coming to *us*."

"But why?" asked Bruno.

"Because they cannot mix with us. They must stay together with other **Jews**."

"Jews," said Bruno. He liked the word. "So the people behind the fence are Jews?"

"That's right."

"Are we Jews?"

Gretel's mouth opened wide. "No, Bruno," she said. "We are not."

"Then what are we?"

"We are the opposite," she answered, quickly. "Yes, that's right. The opposite."

"Don't the Jews like the opposite then?"

"No, it's us who don't like them, stupid." But as she was saying it, she was discovering something strange in her hair.

"Well, can't someone just get us together and . . . "

But Bruno was stopped by a loud scream which brought their mother running to the bedroom. Gretel lifted her finger and showed Mother a very small egg. "It was in my hair!" she said.

"Oh, I don't believe it," said Mother. "But something like this *had* to happen in this dirty place."

Both Bruno and Gretel had **lice** in their hair. Gretel used some special lice **shampoo** on her hair which smelt horrible. Bruno used the shampoo, too, but then Father decided it was easiest to **shave** his hair **off**.

Later Bruno looked at himself in a mirror and felt ill. His face looked strange and ugly, but he also looked like Shmuel. "Did the people on the other side of the fence have lice, too?" he thought. "Is that why their heads are shaved?"

———

When he looked at his friend the next day, Shmuel laughed at him.

"I look just like you now," said Bruno, sadly.

"Only fatter," replied Shmuel.

Leaving Out-With

During the next few weeks, Mother became more and more unhappy. Bruno thought he understood why. She had no one to talk to after Lieutenant Kotler left. She needed a friend like Shmuel.

One day when Bruno was passing Father's office, he heard his parents talking.

"It's horrible," Mother was saying. "Really horrible. I don't want to be here any more."

"We have to be here," said Father. "This is my work . . . "

"Yes, this is *your* work," snapped Mother. "Not ours. You can stay here if you want."

Bruno did not hear much more because the voices were getting close to the door, so he ran upstairs. But he knew that the family might go back to Berlin. He was not sure how he felt about that now.

Nothing changed for a few weeks. Then one day, Father called Bruno and Gretel to his office.

"Sit down, children," he said, sitting behind his desk. "We've decided to make some changes," he continued, looking a bit sad. "Tell me, are you happy here?"

"Yes, Father, of course," said Gretel.

"Very happy," said Bruno.

"And you don't miss Berlin at all?"

The children were quiet for a moment. Then Gretel said, "Well, actually, I miss it terribly. I'd like to have some friends again."

Bruno smiled and thought about his secret.

"Friends, yes . . ." said Father. Then he turned to Bruno. "And you Bruno? Do you miss your friends?"

"Well, yes," he replied, carefully. "But I think that I will always miss people when I go somewhere new."

"Your mother wants to go back to Berlin," Father said. "And she's right. You've been here too long. I will stay here because my work must continue. But it's time for you both to go home."

When Bruno went to tell Shmuel his news the next day, his friend was not there. He was not there the following day or the one after that either. But on the fourth day the boy in the striped pyjamas was back again.

Bruno smiled and sat down on the ground opposite him. Then he held out a piece of bread from the kitchen. Shmuel usually reached quickly for any food which Bruno brought, but today he did not. And he looked even more unhappy.

"I thought that you weren't coming any more," said Bruno. "I came yesterday and the day before, and you weren't here."

"I'm sorry," said Shmuel. "Something happened."

"What was it?" asked Bruno.

"It's Father. I can't find him," replied Shmuel.

"You can't find him? That's very strange. Maybe he went to work in a different place?"

"I hope so," said Shmuel.

"I could ask Father. He knows lots about life on your side of the fence."

"I don't think that is a very good idea," said Shmuel.

"Why?"

"Because the soldiers hate us and we hate them."

Bruno sat back in surprise. "You don't hate Father, do you?"

Shmuel said nothing. He often saw Bruno's father and did not understand how a bad man like the Commandant could have a nice son like Bruno.

"Anyway, I have something to tell you," said Bruno.

"You do?" said Shmuel with hope in his eyes.

"Yes, I'm going back to Berlin. Mother doesn't like it at Out-With."

Shmuel's mouth opened in surprise. "Are you?" he said. "When?"

"Well, this is Thursday," said Bruno. "And we're leaving on Saturday. After lunch. I think it will be for ever. Father is staying because he has to work, but Gretel, Mother and I are going home."

"So I won't see you again?" said Shmuel.

"One day, yes," said Bruno. "You can come on holiday to Berlin. You can't stay here for ever, can you?"

Shmuel shook his head. "No, I can't." Then he said, "I won't have anyone to talk to after you've gone."

"No," said Bruno. "So tomorrow will be the last time we'll be together until you come to Berlin," he continued. "I'll bring you some nice food."

Shmuel nodded, but he looked very sad and could not speak.

"I've always wanted to come and see what it's like on your side of the fence. So we could play together. We never have," said Bruno.

"Well, why don't you then?" said Shmuel.

Bruno thought for a moment, then he took the wire and pulled it up. "But there will be trouble if someone finds me," he said, looking up at Shmuel. "Father will not be happy."

Both boys were quiet for a few moments. Then Bruno suddenly had an idea. He pointed to his shaved head. "What if . . . " he began. "You think that I look like you now, don't you? Now my head is shaved?"

"But you're fatter," said Shmuel.

"Well, if you can find me a pair of striped pyjamas, too, then I can come and visit, and no one will know."

Shmuel suddenly smiled widely. "There's a shed which is full of pyjamas," he said. "Really? Will you come? You can help me to look for Father."

"Why not?" said Bruno. "We can go exploring and see if we can find him."

"Then it's a plan," said Shmuel. "We'll meet at the same time tomorrow."

"Don't be late this time," said Bruno, standing up. "And don't forget the striped pyjamas."

CHAPTER TWELVE
Together at last

The next day it rained. Bruno watched it coming down hard outside the window during his lessons with Herr Liszt. It was still raining heavily at lunch time, but luckily it stopped when Herr Liszt was leaving. Bruno got a pair of boots and a heavy raincoat and then left the house.

When he reached Shmuel, the sky was still dark but there was no rain. Shmuel was standing for a change.

"Hello, Bruno," he said, when he saw his friend coming. "I wasn't sure if you were coming."

"Hello, Shmuel. Yes, I wasn't sure either."

Then Shmuel put out his hands and showed Bruno a pair of dirty striped pyjamas and a cloth cap.

"Do you still want to help me find Father?" he said and Bruno nodded quickly.

Then Shmuel lifted the bottom of the fence and passed the clothes to Bruno, who put them on. He did not have a bag for his other clothes so he had to put them on the wet mud. "This is like being in one of Grandmother's plays," he said, smiling and turning around in circles.

"You need to take off your boots," said Shmuel. "No one wears them in here and they will know that you are different."

Bruno sighed but he knew that his friend was right. He took off the boots and left them next to the clothes.

At first it felt horrible putting his feet in the mud, but then he started to enjoy it.

Then Shmuel lifted the fence and Bruno lay down and pushed himself under it. When he stood up on the other side, he had mud all over his pyjamas, and it felt wonderful.

The boys both smiled. Bruno wanted to put his arms around Shmuel, but something stopped him. Shmuel felt the same. He wanted to thank Bruno for coming to see him and bringing him food. And for helping him to look for Father.

Together they started walking towards the long buildings. It did not take long to reach them. Bruno's eyes opened wide in surprise at what he saw around him. He always **imagined** lots of happy families. He imagined mothers who sat outside in the evenings and told stories to their children. He imagined the children playing games and a shop or café – and maybe even a fruit and vegetable market.

But the truth was very different. No one was sitting outside the buildings telling stories, and the children were not playing. There were only crowds of people standing or sitting together in striped pyjamas, looking at the ground. They were all very thin and they all looked very, very sad.

In one corner, Bruno could see three soldiers. They were watching about twenty men in striped pyjamas. They were shouting at them and some of the men kept falling down with their heads in their arms. In another corner, he could see more soldiers standing with guns under their arms and laughing. They kept pointing the guns at different people.

"I don't think that I like it here," said Bruno.

"I don't like it either," said Shmuel.

"I think that I should go home."

Shmuel stopped walking and looked at him. "But you promised to help me find Father," he said.

Bruno thought about it. "I did promise you, you're right," he said. "Let's keep looking."

The two boys walked around the buildings. They did not know what they were looking for, but Bruno was happy to be exploring.

But they did not find Shmuel's Father and soon the sky began to turn very dark. "I think it might rain again," said Bruno. "I should go home. I'm sorry we haven't found him."

Shmuel nodded his head sadly. He was not really surprised because he did not expect to find his father. He opened his mouth to answer, but at that moment one of the soldiers shouted. Then ten soldiers came to the area of the camp where Bruno and Shmuel were standing.

"What's happening?" said Bruno.

"It happens sometimes," replied Shmuel. "They make people go on **marches**."

"Marches?" said Bruno, frowning. "I can't go on a march! I have to get home. We have chicken for dinner tonight!"

"Be quiet!" said Shmuel. "Don't say anything or they will get angry."

Bruno was happy that all the people in the striped pyjamas were standing together now and he and Shmuel were in the middle. The soldiers could not see them. But Bruno did not understand why everyone looked so frightened. He wanted to tell them that everything was fine, that Father was the Commandant. If he wanted them to go on marches, then it had to be all right.

There was another shout and then everyone began to **march** slowly with Bruno and Shmuel still in the middle.

"Do the marches last for a long time?" Bruno whispered to Shmuel, because he was feeling quite hungry now.

"I don't think so," replied Shmuel. "I never see the people after the marches. But I don't think they do."

Bruno looked up at the black sky. It was beginning to rain heavily again. He could feel the wet mud on his body and his pyjamas were now very wet. He wanted very much to be back in his house watching from his bedroom window.

"That's enough," he said to Shmuel. "I'm going home."

But as he said this, he felt steps under his feet, and suddenly the group of people were marching down into a long room with no windows. It was very warm and dry.

"Well, that's good," he said, happy to be out of the rain. "I expect we'll wait here until the rain stops and then I'll go home. I'm sorry we didn't find your father."

"It's all right," said Shmuel.

"And I'm sorry we didn't play, but we will when you come to Berlin. And you can meet – oh, what were their names?" But he could not remember any of his friends' names or their faces.

Then he did something surprising. He reached down and held Shmuel's hand.

"You're my best friend, Shmuel," he said. "My best friend for life."

But Bruno did not hear what Shmuel replied because at that moment there were loud shouts as the door to the room was closed. "Maybe it's to stop the rain from coming in," Bruno thought.

Then everything went dark. Bruno kept holding Shmuel's hand and even when everyone began to scream, he knew that he must never stop holding it.

———

No one saw Bruno again after that. They looked around the house and went to the village with pictures of the little boy, but no one knew where he was.

A few days later, one of the soldiers found his clothes and boots by the fence, and went to get the Commandant. Bruno's father looked around the area and along the fence, but he did not find his son.

Mother did not go back to Berlin immediately. She stayed at Out-With for three months waiting for news of Bruno. Then one day she suddenly thought, "Maybe he went back to Berlin?" She took Gretel and quickly went back to the city. He was not there, of course.

Gretel threw away her maps and newspapers and stayed in her room and cried. She was not sad because she left her dolls at Out-With, but because she missed Bruno so much.

Father stayed at Out-With for another year, but the other soldiers stopped liking him because he shouted a lot and was always angry. He went to bed every night thinking about Bruno and woke up thinking about him. One day he had an idea about what happened to his son. He went back to the place where the clothes were found the year before. Then he noticed the broken wire and lifted it, and saw that there was a hole big enough for a boy to get through. He looked at the long wooden buildings and then imagined Bruno's journey towards them. Suddenly his legs did not seem to be working, and then he was sitting on the ground.

A few months after that, some other soldiers came to Out-With and Father had to leave with them. He went silently, because he did not care what they did to him.

———

And that is the end of the story about Bruno and his family. Of course, this was a long time ago and nothing like this could ever happen again, could it?

During-reading questions

Write the answers to these questions in your notebook.

CHAPTER ONE

1 Who is "the Fury"? Why does Bruno think he is rude?
2 Who has told Bruno that Gretel "WAS A LOT OF
   TROUBLE FROM THE BEGINNING."?
3 What happens after Hitler's visit?

CHAPTER TWO

1 How is the new house different to the old one in Berlin?
2 What do Gretel and Bruno see out of the window?
3 *"They were everyone."* What does the writer mean, do you think?
   What does Gretel notice next that makes this sentence wrong?

CHAPTER THREE

1 What does Bruno's father say about the people behind the
   fence? What does he mean, do you think?
2 "He is a good man," says Maria about Bruno's father.
   Why does she say this?
3 What do the soldiers and Bruno say and do when they leave
   Bruno's father's office?

CHAPTER FOUR

1 What does Bruno think about Lieutenant Kotler?
2 Why doesn't Bruno need to see a doctor?
3 Why does Bruno's mother say to Pavel, "We'll say that
   I cleaned Bruno's cut."?

CHAPTER FIVE

1 What do Bruno and his Grandmother do every Christmas?
2 Why was Grandmother angry with her son, do you think?

CHAPTER SIX

1 What things are the same between Shmuel and Bruno? What things are different?
2 What parts of Shmuel's journey to Out-With were the same as Bruno's, in Bruno's eyes?
3 Why doesn't Bruno tell the family about Shmuel, do you think?

CHAPTER SEVEN

1 How does Shmuel feel about Lieutenant Kotler?
2 Why does Bruno's father ask Lieutenant Kotler questions about his father? How does Lieutenant Kotler feel about these questions, do you think?
3 What does Pavel do and what happens next, do you think?

CHAPTER EIGHT

1 The people behind the fence wear the same striped clothes. How does Shmuel explain this?
2 How does Bruno tell Gretel about Shmuel, but keep his friend a secret?
3 Why does Gretel think that Bruno must not tell his father about his imaginary friend?

CHAPTER NINE

1 Why is Shmuel in the kitchen?
2 "I've never seen him in my life. I don't know him," says Bruno about Shmuel. Why does he say this, do you think?
3 What will happen to Shmuel now, do you think?

CHAPTER TEN

1 Why does Gretel think that the Jews are behind the fence?
2 Why does Gretel scream?
3 Why does Bruno's father shave Bruno's head?

CHAPTER ELEVEN

1 Why does mother become more and more unhappy, do you think?
2 Why doesn't Shmuel come to meet Bruno for three days?
3 What plan do the two boys make for the next day?

CHAPTER TWELVE

1 Why don't the soldiers at Out-With notice Bruno?
2 How are the people behind the fence different from the way Bruno imagined them?
3 How does Bruno's father feel at the end of the story, do you think?

After-reading questions

1 Which character changes most in the story, do you think? How do they change and why?
2 Why did Lieutenant Kotler leave Out-With, do you think?
3 *The Boy in the Striped Pyjamas* is told through the eyes of Bruno, who is a child. Is the story better than if it was told by an adult? Why/Why not?
4 "Of course, this was a long time ago and nothing like this could ever happen again, could it?" writes the author. What does he mean, do you think?

Exercises

CHAPTER ONE

1 Are these sentences *true* or *false*? Write the correct answers in your notebook.

1 Bruno remembers the Fury coming to dinner. ....*true*....
2 The Fury is the leader of France.
3 The Fury likes speaking French.
4 Bruno likes the Fury.
5 Bruno's family are leaving Berlin.
6 Maria is Bruno's sister.

CHAPTER TWO

2 Match the words with their definitions in your notebook.

| miss | sort out | prepare | wire | pyjamas |

1 a long piece of very thin metal ....*wire*.........
2 to make something ready
3 to feel sad because someone is not with you
4 to put things in their correct place or into groups
5 trousers and a shirt that you wear in bed

CHAPTER THREE

3 Complete the sentences in your notebook with the correct form of the verb.

1 Bruno saw his father ....*standing*.... (**stand**) with a group of five men.
2 Father .... (**sit**) behind the desk and he looked up from some papers when Bruno entered.

3 "Ah, *those* people," said Father, nodding again because now he .... (**understand**).

4 Then he .... (**lift**) his arm in the air and said those two important words.

5 A few days later, Bruno was .... (**lie**) on his bed and looking at the dirty walls in his bedroom.

6 But the sound of a car door .... (**close**) made her silent.

CHAPTER FOUR

4 Who is thinking this, do you think? Write the correct names in your notebook.

1 "I'm really bored." ..... *Bruno* .....

2 "I like talking to this handsome young man. I want my brother to leave us."

3 "I will ask that dirty — to help Bruno."

4 "He is hurt. I am a doctor and I must help him."

5 "I must not tell my husband about this."

6 "How can Pavel be a doctor *and* a waiter?"

CHAPTER FIVE

5 Which word is closest in meaning? Write the correct word in your notebook.

1 uniform	hair	*clothes*	body
2 handsome	plain	ugly	good-looking
3 play	drawing	acting	exploring
4 tutor	student	teacher	singer
5 history	future	now	past

6 **Write the question tags in your notebook.**

1 Gretel did not want to play with Bruno, ...*did she*..... ?

2 Bruno loved exploring, ... ?

3 The small dark thing was a boy, ... ?

4 The boy wasn't very happy, ... ?

5 The young boys fought a lot, ... ?

6 Bruno didn't have any food, ... ?

7 **Write the questions to these answers in your notebook.**

1 *Why was Bruno late?*

    Because he was talking to Maria.

2 Because he lives on Shmuel's side of the fence.

3 He wants to work in a zoo.

4 He taught art at a university.

5 Pavel dropped wine on his legs.

6 No, no one tried to stop him.

8 **Put the sentences in the correct order in your notebook.**

a .... A few days later it was raining heavily.

b .....*1*..... One afternoon, Bruno noticed a bruise on Shmuel's eye.

c .... Gretel came to Bruno's room.

d .... Bruno told Gretel about his imaginary friend.

e .... Bruno tried to read a book.

f .... Shmuel didn't want to talk about it.

9 **Match the two parts of these sentences in your notebook.**

Example: 1–c

1 When they did meet, Bruno worried that

2 Bruno walked into the kitchen feeling very angry,

3 Bruno did not want to look at Shmuel's hand any more, so

4 Shmuel quickly reached for another glass

5 He turned back to Shmuel,

a and began cleaning it.

b he went to the fridge and opened it.

c his friend was getting thinner and thinner.

d who was looking at the floor.

e and suddenly he got the biggest surprise of his life.

10 **Write the correct names in your notebook.**

1 She died suddenly so the family went home. ......*Grandmother*......

2 He left Out-With after a lot of shouting between Mother and Father.

3 She became more and more unhappy and wanted to go home to Berlin.

4 She misses her friends in Berlin terribly.

5 He cannot find his father.

CHAPTER TWELVE

11 **Write the correct question words. Then answer the questions in your notebook.**

1 ..*When*.. did it stop raining?
   It stopped raining when Herr Liszt was leaving.

2 .... did Shmuel give Bruno to wear?

3 .... did Bruno have to take off his boots?

4 .... did Bruno get to Shmuel's side of the fence?

Project work

1 Imagine you are Shmuel. Write a diary of your journey to Out-With.

2 What happened to the Jews and German soldiers at Auschwitz at the end of the Second World War? Look online and make a presentation.

3 Write a letter to Shmuel from Bruno when he goes back to Berlin after his grandmother dies. How does he feel about seeing Berlin and his friends again? How does he feel about leaving Shmuel?

4 Write a different ending to the story.

5 Compare the book to the film of *The Boy in the Striped Pyjamas* (2008). How are they the same/different? Why did the writer make these changes for the film do you think?

An answer key for all questions and exercises can be found at **www.penguinreaders.co.uk**

Glossary

bruise (n.)
a blue, yellow or brown area on your skin where someone or something has hit it

cap (n.)
a small hat

cloth (adj. and n.)
clothes are made of cloth. A cloth cap is soft.

Commandant (n.)
a title for an important soldier

confused (adj.)
You are *confused* when you do not understand what is happening.

exploring (n.); **explorer** (n.)
Exploring is going to places to learn more about them. An *explorer* is a person who does this. An *explorer* *explores* places.

floor (n.)
A *floor* is part of a building. When you go into a building, you are on the ground *floor*. If you go upstairs, you are on the first *floor*, and if you go upstairs again, you are on the second *floor*.

forgive (v.)
to decide that you will not be angry with someone who has hurt you

frown (v.)
to move the top part of your face to show that you are not happy or you are thinking hard

history (n.)
a school subject about all things that happened before now

imaginary (adj.); **imagine** (v.)
imaginary things are not real. You *imagine* them in your *mind*.

Jew (n.)
the Jews are a group of people. After the Second World War, many Jews who were not killed left Europe to live in Israel.

leader (n.)
People follow a *leader*, and they do what their *leader* tells them.

lice (n.)
small insects that can live in people's hair. We say *louse* for one of them.

lift (v.)
to move something up

lonely (adj.)
not happy to be alone

maid (n.)
a woman who cleans rooms and washes clothes in a family's house

march (n. and v.)
When a group of people march, they walk together like soldiers. A *march* is when they do this.

miss (v.)
If you *miss* someone, you feel sad because they are not with you.

mud (n.)
soft, wet ground in a field, for
example

pack (v.)
to put your clothes in bags and
boxes because you are going to
take them somewhere

plaster (n.)
You put a *plaster* on a cut to keep
it clean.

play (n.)
a *play* is when people act a story.
People often watch *plays* in a theatre.

polite (adj.)
When you are *polite* or speak *politely*,
you say things in a nice way.

post (n.)
a tall piece of wood that you put in
the ground. People use *posts* to hold
up a fence.

prepare (v.)
to make something ready

proud (adj.)
Someone who is *proud* sometimes
thinks they are better than other
people.

rope (n.)
You use a long, strong *rope* to pull
something or to hold things together.

rude (adj.)
not acting in a nice way

shampoo (n.)
You use *shampoo* with water to wash
your hair.

shave (off) (v.)
When you *shave* hair *off,* you cut
it all off.

shed (n.)
a building, often made of wood,
in a garden or on a farm

sigh (v.)
to let air out of your mouth slowly
when you are tired or sad

sink (n.)
in a kitchen, you fill a sink with
water to wash cups and plates

snap (v.)
to speak to someone suddenly
in an angry way

sort out (phr. v.)
to put things in their correct place
or into groups

striped (adj.)
Striped clothes have lines on them.

tutor (n.)
someone who teaches students in
their own home

wire (n.)
a long piece of very thin metal.
A *wire fence* is made of wire.

wooden (adj.)
made of wood

Penguin 🐧 **Readers**

Visit **www.penguinreaders.co.uk**
for FREE Penguin Readers resources
and digital and audio versions of this book.